Happ

CW01662486

Hope you enjoy snuggling up with Kit to read these together!

Well-Versed
CATS

Also by Lance Percival
WELL-VERSED DOGS

Well-Versed
CATS

Lance Percival

Illustrated by Lalla Ward

W.H. ALLEN · LONDON

COMET

Copyright © Lance Percival, 1986

Typeset by Phoenix Photosetting, Chatham, Kent
Printed in Great Britain by
Mackays of Chatham Ltd, Chatham, Kent
for the Publishers, W.H. Allen & Co. Plc
44 Hill Street, London W1X 8LB

ISBN 0 491 03005 3 (W.H. Allen Hardcover)
ISBN 0 86379 128 X (Comet Paperback)

This book is sold subject to the condition that it shall not, by way of trade or otherwise, be lent, re-sold, hired out or otherwise circulated without the publisher's prior consent in any other form of binding or cover other than that in which it is published and without a similar condition including this condition being imposed upon the subsequent purchaser.

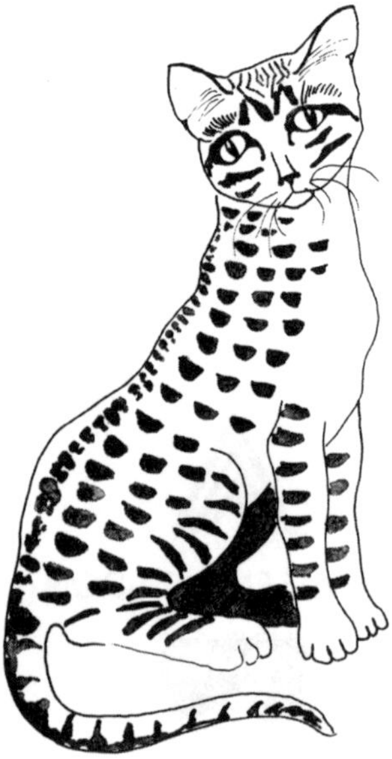

Contents

For Little Jamie
and Tricia the Tiger

The Abyssinian

Two thousand years back on the banks of the Nile there
appeared a strange intruder
Who claimed that he was a pussy cat that was bred by the
Lion of Judah.
He looked a bit like a rabbit, which Egyptians thought
rather funny,
And that's why Abyssinian cats are often referred to as
Bunny.

In modern times they're better known with tufted ears on
their head,
And coppery coats that are russet or even a sex-linked red.
It doesn't matter wherever you live, in the Solomon Isles or
Sardinia,
Whenever you leave they will raise a paw and solemnly purr
'A bee seen ya'.

But Abysinnians are very aware of the money people have
paid,
To fight Ethiopian famine by giving so much to Band Aid.
So they've clubbed together a blanket each and stitched
together a beaut,
They wanted to thank Bob Geldof, and they knew he
needed a suit.

The Alarm Call Cat

Are you awakened each morning
By the shrill of an early alarm?
Which is followed fast by the radio blast;
Efficient, but lacking in charm?

Do you believe in a telephone call?
Just think of the cost of all that;
And think of the noise, no think of the joys
Of being woken each day by my cat.

At a quarter to eight, and he's never been late,
He climbs to the top of my bed.
I can hear him saw as one little paw
Gently taps on my head.

It's a marvellous way to be woken,
Although I should add a warning:
The dear little creep won't allow me to sleep
Until nine on a Sunday morning.

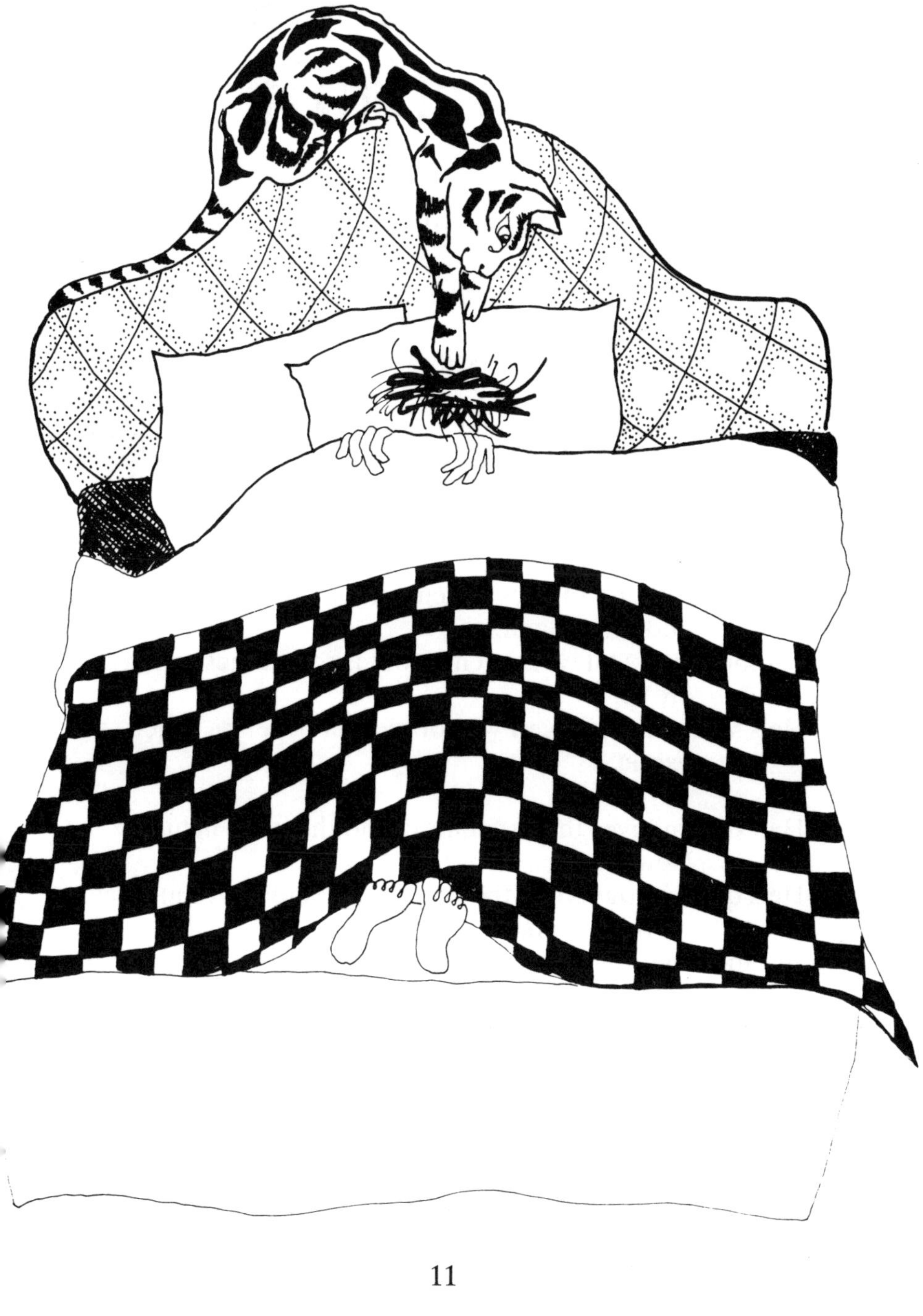

American Exotic Shorthair

The Exotic American Shorthair is really a modified version
Of a plain American Shorthair and a somewhat exotic Persian.
The American genes are easily seen 'cause the cat's always chewing gum,
And the Persian blood is revealed by the thud when he sits on his fluffy bum.

So he lives on burgers and hot dogs, and cookies straight from a jar,
While his other half tries to remember what life was like under the Shah.
Although the 'Alley' cat centrefold is sometimes rather erotic,
He's sure the American way of life can never be called exotic.

Half of him loves the razzmatazz and the neon lights of New York.
He's quite intrigued by the Ivy League and the funny way cowboys walk,
But the other half just sits quietly and tries to remember the dates
Of all the famous victories that were Alexander the Great's.

Cooki
ALEXANDER THE GREAT

The Balinese

You can search old Bali high, you can search old Bali low
But you'll never find a Balinese cat over there you know.
They were bred in the United States and when they started prancing
The breeder said their movements were like Bali ladies dancing.

The ladies there are lovely, but the breeder, Mr Mahler,
Actually saw their movements in a Bali massage parlour,
And though the girls are very skilled at being a rubber dubber,
The cat is not related to a naughty Bali scrubber.

The Balinese have silky coats that daily must be groomed,
And a most distinguished tail which is best described as plumed.
They love to play and frolic, so much so you can be certain,
That you'll hear the noisy rip as they zip straight up your curtain.

Even so a Balinese may be your favourite choice,
Until of course, you're witness to the shrillness of her voice.
Her caterwaul's so piercing, it's enough to make you blubber,
The one thing that she has in common with a Bali scrubber.

The Birman

In an ancient Burmese temple an old priest used to pray
To the Golden Goddess with the sapphire eyes.
She was also worshipped by 100 pure white cats,
Till Infidels attacked them with surprise.

When the priest was slain a cat leapt on his back
And faced the Goddess, praying with all his might.
His eyes turned sapphire blue and his legs went brownish
too,
But the bottom of his feet stayed solid white.

The Infidels all fled, and if you think you've read
A phony story, find some Birman kittens.
They may be roly poly and not appear too holy,
But every single one will have white mittens.

The Bombay Bomber

If you ever cop a cat with glowing copper eyes,
A black panther coat, and his hackles start to rise,
Be very, very careful what you do and what you say,
'Cause you are face to face with the Bomber from Bombay.

The Bomber from Bombay is a tiny little mite,
But he makes up for his size with a hefty appetite.
He'll gobble down a Bindi Gusht, a Chicken Vindaloo,
A Bombay Duck, a Poppadum and Onion Bhajee too.

Next he has Tandoori, plus a fairly spicy curry,
And when he has digested that, he gets up in a hurry,
Nips outside and crouches down with dignified aplomb,
And you'll discover where the Bomber got his nickname
from!

The British Shorthair

The British Shorthair cat wants to make it very clear
That it doesn't want no European Short 'Airs over 'ere.
'E ain't too keen on Persians or the Siamese persuasion,
And is very, very anti any Burmese Brown invasion.

And as for Russian Blues or any Abysinnian kitten,
'E doesn't think that cats like that should be allowed in
Britain.
'E reckons that his neighbourhood is getting rather shabby
And far too full of Chinks like the Oriental Tabby.

'E vows 'e's going to stop all this foreign immigration,
By making 'em all subject to immediate deportation.
Any foreign cats who try to start an 'urly burly,
The Short 'Airs going to grab 'em by the very short and
curly!

The Bronze Egyptian Mau

The Bronze Egyptian Mau in history is slotted
As the one cat in the world that is naturally spotted.
He also must have frown marks, but you'll know the perfect gem,
When right across his forehead you see the letter 'M'.

The 'M', of course, denotes that he's the boss of young James Bond –
You must recall Bronzefinger, of which I'm very fond –
He's served as 'M' for many years, the Bronze Egyptian Mau,
But he'll never be as elderly as Roger Moore is now!

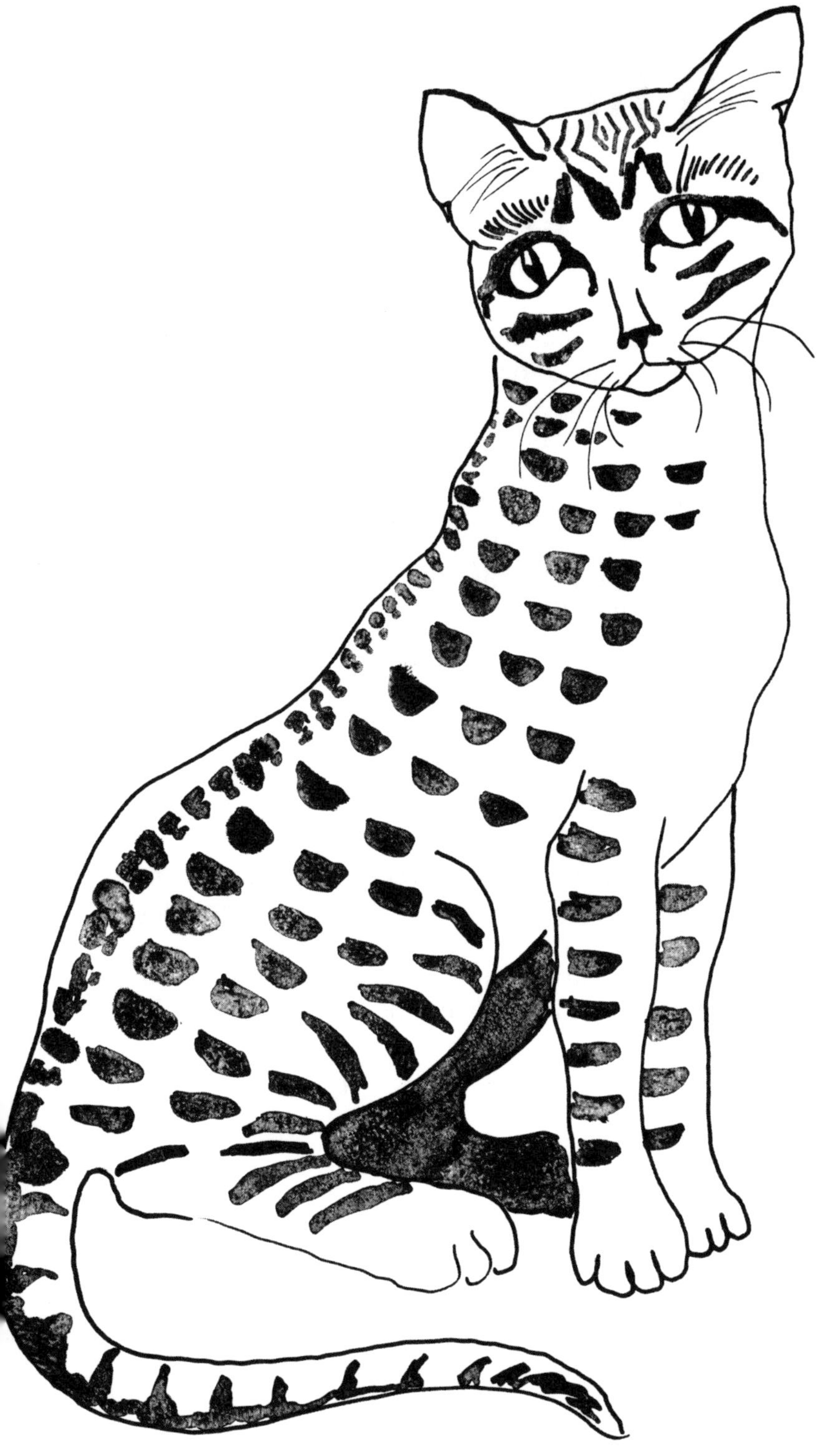

The Burmese Brown

In the streets of old Rangoon, way back in 1930
Lived a cat with golden eyes till someone did the dirty,
And took her to the USA hoping to succeed
In starting a new strain if the cat would interbreed.

The culprit's name was Thompson, a doctor in the navy,
Who patently loved any cats whose colouring was gravy.
But breeding cats called Thompson somehow didn't gel.
In Africa the 'non-P' Thomsons had their own gazelle.

Meanwhile in the States, she was difficult to please
Refused to try and mate with a 'common' Siamese.
After clawing two, she announced 'I'll get much firmer
Unless someone brings a ruddy great big brown tom cat
from Burma'.

Eventually the tom arrived and soon the kittens came . . .
Wang Mau was very happy – yes that was the mother's
name.
But before you start to run the deeds of Thompson down,
Remember that he left us with the lovely Burmese Brown.

Catholic Kate

Kate the cat was a *Cat*holic
With a touch of Puritanism.
She knelt by a *cat*erpillar in church
And recited her *cat*echism.

So when a *cat*astrophe killed her
The *cat*hedral was filled with gloom;
And at her request, she was laid to rest
In the bowels of a *Cat*acomb.

The choir, in harmony, *cat*erwauled
The Virgin's Magnifi*cat*.
The Vicar's surprise was to *cat*egorise
Young Kate as a virginal cat.

He preached 'Young Kate has been through nine lives
But also nine Tom Cats as well –
And if you do that, even though you're a cat
You'll be *cat*apulted to Hell'.

Catmint

You can grow what you like in your garden
With one exception – Catmint,
Because if you do and your cat has a chew,
He'll develop a nasty squint.

He will then do two backward somersaults
And walk straight into the fence;
Next he'll be raving about his craving
For Catmint, which doesn't make sense.

A cat can eat Spearmint no bother
And Peppermint all the way through,
But he'll come to grief on a Catmint leaf
And a bit of a Varmint too.

So Rosemary, Basil, the Thyme has arrived
To be Sage about herbs you can grow.
A cat really thrives on Parsley and Chives,
But Catmint must certainly go.

Cat-O-Nine-Lives

Everyone knows that a cat has nine lives
And the detail of each never pales,
But if he whips round to tell you all nine
He's known as a Cat-o-Nine-Tales.

Cats in the Rain

Standing soaked in the High Street,
London weather cold and drab,
No sign of a double decker,
No sign of a Taxi cab,

No sign of a raincoat either –
I forgot to bring it out.
In a book of well-versed pussies,
What's this poem all about?

By the time my shoes are soggy
In the sleet my memory jogs:
'No use, mate, in *hailing* Taxis
When it's *raining* cats and dogs'.

Cats v. Dogs

Dogs will come when you whistle,
Or bark at a knock on the door,
Retrieve old sticks or learn new tricks,
Or lie by your feet on the floor.

Cats of course can do all of those things
In a manner that's highly resplendent,
But never show skill when you hope they will,
'Cause by nature they're most independent.

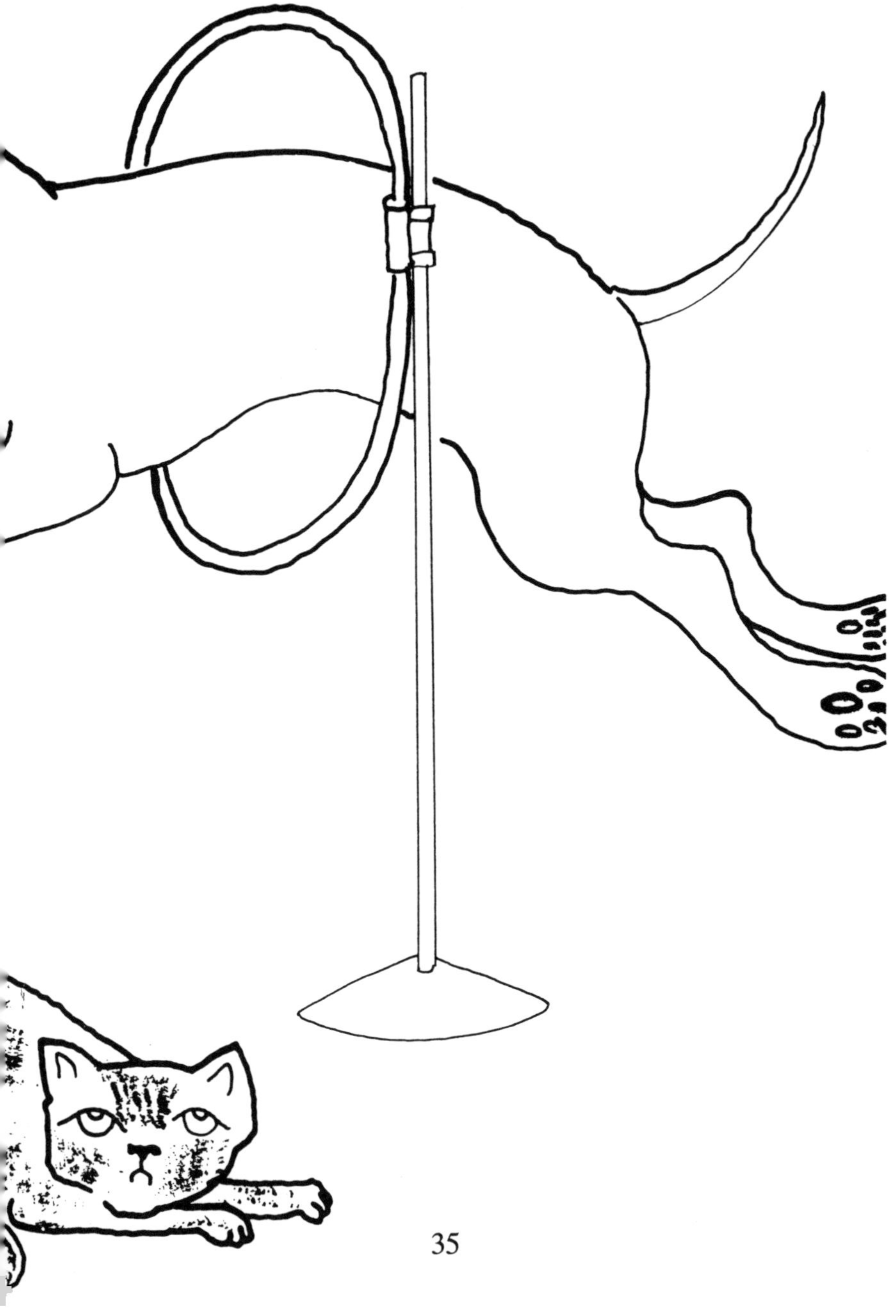

Chartreux Blue

If you're looking for a rare cat, try the short hair Chartreux Blue,
They're bred by old Carthusian monks with nothing else to do;
But if you give her common milk, you'll find this Blue prefers
The somewhat more expensive taste of lapping Green Chartreuse!

MILK

The Christmas Kitten

I was glancing in a shop window
At a Holy Nativity scene
When suddenly a kitten appeared
Where the stable door had been.

She tiptoed softly through the straw
Looking a little weary,
But being very small she managed to squeeze
In between Joseph and Mary.

She wisely avoided the Three Wise Men
And after removing the bib,
She gently picked up the baby child
And nestled herself in the crib.

None of the passers-by noticed
The motionless furry stranger,
But having a kitten is better by far
Than having a dog in the manger.

Coco the Korat Kitten

The Korat cat has alert green eyes and a coat that is silver blue,
And the female Korats are highly renowned as very good mothers too.
They say that spotting a Korat is a sign of very good luck,
But they also say that Korat kittens look like an ugly duck.

Coco the Korat kitten soon noticed that every day,
Anyone seeing him, human or cat, immediately turned away.
He managed to find a mirror, which left him extremely glum.
Why was Coco so ugly, compared to the beauty of Mum?

At first he reasoned his dad must have been an out-of-town alley cat moggie,
Or even a passing mongrel, as he looked decidedly doggy.
Try as he might to be friendly, the neighbouring cats all spat
'Get out of my way you half breed git, you're obviously not a Korat'.

After two years of insults, he was feeling decidedly blue,
Till one day he noticed his mangy hair was beginning to go blue too.
The transformation was sudden and he no longer feels inferior,
For Coco the Korat kitten is the handsomest cat in the area.

The moral of this saga which your knowledge should
envelop,
Is the beauty of Korat kittens takes at least 2 years to
develop.
So if you consider you're rather plain, no need to worry and
fret:
Remember the Korat kittens, there may be hope for you
yet!

The Comma and the Cat

When you were a toddler were you taught by your Momma,
The difference that exists between a cat and a comma?
A comma has a pause at the end of its clause,
While a cat has its claws on its paws!

Grammar
for
beginners

Cornish Rex Mawgan

Mawgan has the markings of a champion Cornish Rex;
Curly coat and Roman nose but also too much sex.
Everybody knows it's true a cat has got nine lives,
But Mawgan's got nine wives as well from Truro to St Ives.

He wanted to preserve his breed by having lots of kittens,
But Cornish winters get so cold he took to wearing mittens.
And Cornish Rex has such short hair, he paid an awful cost,
He lost his ears and tail to a very heavy frost.

Earless, tailess Mawgan is a sorry, sorry sight,
As he trudges off to Penryn on a freezing, frosty night.
He heard there was a beauty queen in season without sex,
And Mawgan was determined to prolong the Cornish Rex.

So if you visit Lizard Point or even far Land's End,
And spot an earless cat who has nothing on his end,
Gently call out 'Mawgan', and then if he turns his face
You're looking at the saviour of the Cornish Rexy Race.

The Curious Cat

At 4 a.m. the cat heard a sound,
So into the night she stole
And found two humans out in the road,
Next to a dirty great hole.

She didn't know they were Gas men
Determined to find a leak;
But when they'd finished their digging about,
She decided to take a peek.

She thought she saw something moving,
And being a curious cat,
She plunged down eight feet into the hole
And on to the back of a rat.

Meanwhile the workmen returned to the hole
And since they'd finished, they filled it.
So although the cat was smelling a rat,
It was curiosity killed it.

Cymric

The Cymrics are cats without any tails
And also got nothing to do with Wales.
Kumric's the way that you're supposed to pronounce it,
But as it's not Welsh I'm going to denounce it.

The American breeder needs a good belt
For naming this yankee cat after a Celt.
Pinching Welsh names won't get you to heaven,
So Cymrics are banned from crossing the Severn.

SEVERN
BRIDGE
NO bicycles,
mopeds, L-drivers
or pedestrians
positively NO
CYMRIC CATS
BY ORDER

Dirty Charlie

Dirty Charlie's very dirty
Quite a filthy little cat;
Till one dirty day he wandered
Through the local laundromat.

Having climbed inside a porthole
He found a place to nap till dinner,
Then his world went whirling mad
Someone had switched on the spinner.

Clawing on to sheets and hankies
Charlie did his best to grope;
Round and round in rushing water,
Almost drowned in lather soap.

When the damned thing stopped at last
Charlie took a dreadful flyer –
Started whizzing twice as fast;
No wonder it's called a *tumble* drier.

By the time the programme finished
Charlie thought that he was dead.
Tried to mew behind the glass,
With ladies' knickers on his head.

A woman screamed, all hell let loose.
So Charlie quickly fled the scene.
But no one calls him Dirty Charlie,
Now he's known as Mister Clean.

PO

Douglas the Manx Cat

Douglas is a Manx cat; the one without a tail,
And how the Manxes lost it is a somewhat shaggy tale:
When Noah counted all the beasts and thought there were no more,
He cut the Manxes' tails off by slamming shut the door.

So Douglas on the Isle of Man feels a proper chump;
Other cats have swishy tails, but all he's got is rump.
There is a stumpy Manx as well, which Douglas thinks is dumb . . .
I bet you wouldn't like a little knobble on your bum.

On the Isle of Man you'll find Douglas any day,
Somewhere between Castletown and northern Ramsey Bay;
And if by chance you spot him, you should take a photograph,
But when you see his backside, I beg of you don't laugh.

Egyptian Cats

In the days of Ancient Egypt the old Pharoah was a sod,
But he had one saving grace 'cause he made the cat a
God.
Well actually a Goddess but quite why we've never
mastered –
The Goddess was called Bast and the Pharoah was a
bastard.

Cats were bowed to in the streets, so deep was the belief
And when they died they were embalmed with solemnity
and grief.
But nowadays the Cairo Cat must learn the Highway Code.
It takes a minor miracle to get across the road.

E.S.P. Tinker

Tinker is a tabby and his master's name is Tom,
Together they're a very happy pair,
As Tommy strokes his fur little Tinker loves to purr,
To indicate a most contented air.

Tommy's place of work wouldn't let him bring his cat,
So Tinker used to roam their flat instead,
Till one day going to work some driver went berserk,
He skidded and killed poor old Tom stone dead.

The priest said at the funeral that Tom was very kind,
He was loved by fellow men and much revered.
But back in Tommy's flat, there was no sign of the cat,
Tinker had completely disappeared.

Two weeks later he was found inside the funeral ground,
Sitting on Tom's grave which puzzles me.
How did Tinker know exactly where to go,
Is it true that cats have E.S.P.?

TOM
RIP
R.I.P

Famous Cats

The Categoric Hall of Fame
Is very very fussy,
So turn again Dick Whittington
You're treading on your Pussy.

Do not laugh at Miaow Tse Tung,
The Hall of Fame won't wear it,
And if you meet a Cheshire Cat
You'll have to grin and bear it.

Don't consider Tom and Jerry
Childish cartoon trash,
The Hall of Fame reveres Sylvester's
'. . . . . Sssuffering Succotash'.

Disney still has Micky Miaows,
With 1930 roots,
And if you're getting sick of this,
You'll find a Puss in *Boots*!

CATEGORIC HALL OF FAME

Flip the Fussy Eater

My neighbour's cat whose name is Flip, she simply
wouldn't eat
Raw beef or pork or well-cooked heart or even liver meat.
Her owner Fred soon became a most impatient man,
When Flip refused to even lick the contents of a can.

Fred put little biscuits out, but Flip ignored the dish.
Same result with cod and plaice and other types of fish,
Till one day, quite frustrated, he then offered Flip some
Rabbit,
Which did the flipping trick – now she's hooked upon the
habit.

Flip eats only rabbit now, which seems an awful pity
To poor old Fred who's living in the middle of a city.
He bought from all the butchers till they were left with
none,
So Freddie roamed the streets with a loaded 12-bore gun.

Fred soon found that city streets with rabbits aren't infested
And anyway for bearing arms Fred was soon arrested.
And if you think this story is absurd, by all means do,
But I wonder if your cat is a fussy eater too.

Ginger the Tom

Ginger is a Tom, who's an angel in the day,
Nestling on your lap quietly purring away;
Or playing harmless games, in which he seems to revel,
But when the sun goes down, he's a dirty little devil.

When he starts his night patrol he's suddenly superior,
And God help any other Tom that strolls into his area.
First he'll scratch their eyes out, then claw the little brats
For entering the Kingdom of Ginger's lady cats.

Ginger chases lady cats even if they're spayed,
And makes sure that their homes are completely Ginger
sprayed.
The owners loathe the smell, but he doesn't care at all,
As he hails the local lovelies with his sexy caterwaul.

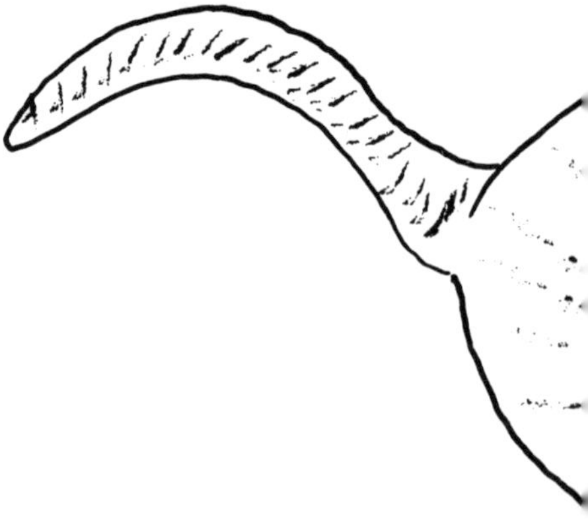

Although they know it's Ginger, it's impossible to prove;
No one's caught him at it, cause he's always on the move.
The only sign of evidence that he's committed sin,
Is the lady cats involved wear a deep, contented grin.

He comes back in the morning when the whole street's been patrolled;
The neighbours tell his owners that 'Your tom should be controlled'.
But if you ask the lady cats every one is smitten,
And you will find a ginger tinge in every single kitten.

Havana Brown

I have a cat who's called José from the breed Havana
Brown,
Whose colour is by far the warmest chocolate brown in
town.
Burmese by descent and rather Siamese in manner,
Havana Browns have, sadly, no connections with Havana.

Presuming that's the truth, will you please explain to me,
Why José always pricks his ears when Fidel Castro's on
TV?
And also after dinner, when I'm passing round cigars,
Why José never smokes them unless they're Bolivars?

BOLIVAR

The Himalayan Colourpoint

The Himalayan Colourpoint's a perfect little pet
But sad to say, their origins are nowhere near Tibet;
It wasn't in the mountains that these longhairs learnt to thrive;
It was Harvard University in 1935.

They mated various Siamese with silver tabby Persians,
And several litters later they were pleased with their exertions.
They took one to a Cat Show, where he pulverised the joint
With his Ivory Persian body and his lovely Chocolate-Point.

Nowadays the Himalayans all look frightfully swish,
Everyone adores them, but they have a sacred wish.
Their wish is very simple, but impossible as yet . . .
To join the Dalai Lama when he goes back to Tibet.

The Jaguar

The Jaguar's the prowler of the southern U.S.A.,
Where she's either climbing mountains or she's
cornering her prey.
The Texan boys are bragging 'She's the neatest cat by far
And it's 'bout time yu-all Limeys made a decent motor car'.

Jeeves the Sophisto Cat

He studies the ads in 'Mouse and Garden'
Before he goes hunting a rat,
And when he has eaten, he begs your pardon,
Does Jeeves the Sophisto Cat.

He caterwauls nightly his serenades,
But kittens he turns down flat.
So he only mates with a Queen of Spayeds,
Does Jeeves the Sophisto Cat.

He gleans the headlines he finds out in 'Mewsweek'
And 'Playpuss' for tarty tat;
He contributes to 'Kittens and Bathrooms' too,
Does Jeeves the Sophisto Cat.

He looks the cat's whiskers and terribly sleek,
In his topper, tails and cravat;
There's a photo in 'Harpurrs' every week
Of Jeeves the Sophisto Cat.

MOUSE AND GARDEN

Jock the Scottish Fold

Jock the Scottish Fold is a ruddy mackerel tabby,
Who thinks the National Cat Club's attitude is rather shabby.
Just because his ears fold down, he's banned from being a member
Of the breeds on show in London, at Olympia each December.

Jock's wee face looks sad, but I think you should be told,
It's the natural expression of the bonnie Scottish Fold.
So Jock marched down to London, to remedy this farce,
Pricked his ears and entered in the British Shorthair Class.

The judges came to look at him and nodded in the know.
They all agreed that he should be the Champion of the Show.
Then he dropped his ears and stopped them in their tracks
With 'I'm a Scottish Fold you stupid half-wit Sassenachs'.

BEST OF BREED

Leo the Lion

Leo is the King of Africa's Savannah,
But I feel you ought to know he's a rotten diet planner.
For twenty hours a day you will find him idly dossing,
Hoping that a gnu will approach his zebra crossing.

For all his hearty prowess, it is doubtful as to whether,
He's ever captured more of an ostrich than its feather.
If animals stood still, he'd enjoy a hearty feast,
But he cannot stand the speed of the blasted hartebeest.

So why is it through history there's always been this fuss,
About the dreadful fear of lions eating us?
We are rather slow, (and I hope you won't get queasy)
Compared to deer I fear we're comparatively easy!

Lionesses catch the food and Leo will confide
He does have several wives who are his joy and Pride.
Which may explain why Leo is constantly being nagged,
But also why this shaggy beast looks permanently shagged.

The Lynx

If you're looking for a Lynx in the forest scrub one day,
Before you waste your time, there are two things I should say.
The first is that they sleep all day and only hunt by night,
And secondly, they'll see you first, as they all have super sight.

As far as I can see there is nothing that surpasses
The eyesight of a Lynx (well none of them wear glasses).
In the southern German Forests a Lynx will often glance
At a distant little hare who thinks he's safe in France.

If he glances to the left he can see the Pope in Rome,
A glance the other way reveals St Paul's Cathedral Dome.
Wherever you may be, and whatever you may do
You can bet your bottom dollar that a Lynx is watching you.

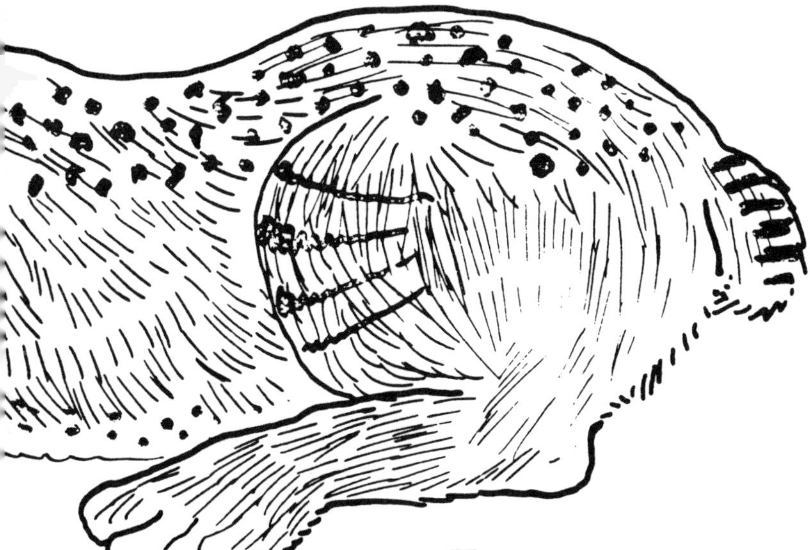

Maine Coon

If ever you should go across the sea to Bangor Maine,
You will find a glowing beauty which you'll never see again.
Just ignore the wooden buildings: I'm afraid they're rather shabby,
Compared to the refinement of the classic Maine Coon tabby.

They claim a male Racoon was so excited he was able
To mate a female cat – very cute but it's a fable.
But in spite of misty origins, one blessing will suffice,
In old New England farms they have killed off all the mice.

They have enormous strength and across their long-haired back
You will find distinctive blotches, nigger brown and nigger black.
But if you don't believe me you should go to Bangor soon,
By all means call them Maine but I would *never* call them Coon!

Miho the Japanese Bobtail

Miho is a Bobtail in a temple of Japan.
Her colouring is mi-ke, and pronounce that if you can.
You might call her tortoise-shell, but never in Japan,
As Miho contemplates the snowy slopes of Fujisan.

For Miho is revered as a wondrous magic charmer;
She sits within the temple of downtown Yokohama.
Europeans think she has her own religious sect,
As pilgrims come from Tokyo to pay her their respect.

But Miho's not a Goddess who is worthy of esteem;
The reason for her presence is quite simple, it would seem:
The priests insist on keeping her within their holy house,
'Cause in their Shinto Temple, you will never find a mouse.

Misty the Talking Cat

Clarissa's cat is Misty,
A lovely Siamese Grey
Who tries to talk by whining,
But what's she trying to say?

She's just been out and just been fed,
This whining is absurd.
Clarissa tries but really doesn't
Understand a word.

Clarissa has a baby girl,
Young Charlie is her name,
And comprehending Charlie's whine
Is practically the same.

So Misty and young Charlie sit
And whine at one another.
And strange to say I think that they
Both understand each other.

The Moggie's Floosie

In Uncle Tom's Bar, taking slugs from a jar
Of very non-vintage Muscat,
Sat a rough looking moggie, who felt a bit groggy,
He saw her and smelt a big rat.

Semi-spayed Floosie, decidedly boozy,
Making catty remarks about sin,
She sexily sighed, but the moggie replied,
'God, look what the cat's brought in'.

She said, feeling chronic, from Gin Catatonic
'Would you care to curl up with me maybe?'
He said 'What a drag, you filthy kitbag,
Not a cat in all hell's chance, baby'.

When she persisted, the moggie insisted
'My dear you've been at it too long . . .
But since you are feline, we might make a bee line
For the cathouse where you belong'.

So they both went back to her tin covered shack
And climbed on the top for the proof,
That the way the cat jumps provides lots of bumps,
For a Cat on a Hot Tin Roof!

Moles

If ever you find that nasty moles
Are digging up your lawn,
Then put a cat beside the mounds
And he'll keep watch till dawn.

Occasionally a horrible mole,
Will pop up through the floor,
And when the little head pokes out,
He'll whack it with his paw.

He'll very seldom eat it.
On moles, a cat won't thrive,
And cats are no damned use at hunting
Moles in MI5.

Catching moles in MI5
Is quite a different chore.
You'll have to telephone James Bond
And ask for Pussy Galore.

My Cat Timothy

Timothy, Timothy can you explain,
I let you out, you come straight back again.
Is it too cold for you to feel bold,
Or are you like me, feeling old?

Timothy, Timothy I go to bed.
Why won't you lie on your blanket instead?
You'll never rest until you can nest
In a round little ball on my chest.

Timothy, Timothy, what would you do
If I was the one to die before you?
I hope that I'm not, I love you a lot,
And remember I'm all that you've got.

Myrtle's Central Heating

If our home is *very* cold
Myrtle can't stand it at all.
She'll lie on the floor and curl right up
Into a tiny ball.

If our home is *fairly* warm
It's still too cold for Myrtle.
She'll wrap herself half way round
Into a semi circle.

If our home is *really* warm
With central heating galore,
Myrtle lies contented, sprawled
Right across the floor.

So if you think your heating's low
Don't check the thermostat,
It's easier by far to check
The *standing* of your cat!

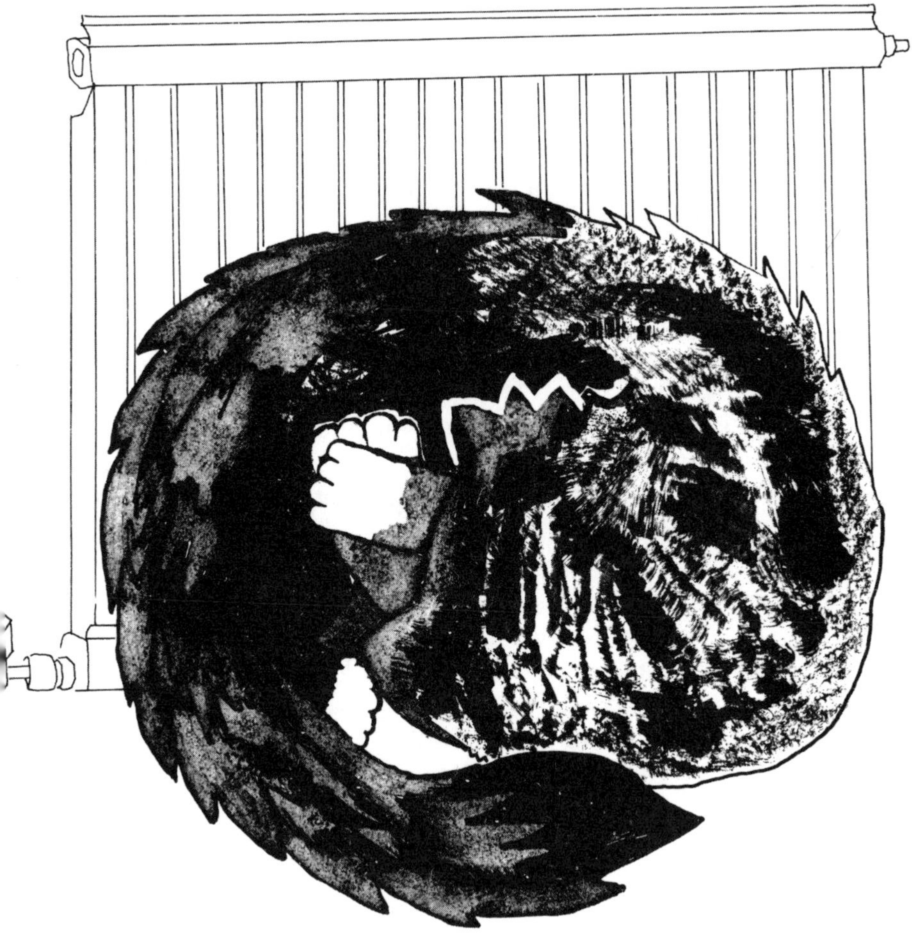

Norwegian Forest Cat

Norway is famous for beautiful Fjords and for people imbibing one drink
But if they then drive, it's 'breathe into this' – and the rest of the week's in the clink,
But when it comes to resisting the cold and a cunning far worse than a rat;
Norwegians swear not a thing will compare to their Torbie and White Forest Cat.

It can shin up a tree like lightning and the craggiest mountains as well.
The foresters call it the Fairy Cat on account of its magical spell.
Expose your hands in the winter out there, you'll suffer from hard frost bite,
But it won't affect the more circumspect Norwegian Torbie and White.

How do they thrive or even survive in the depths of Norwegian snow?
And try as we might, the Torbie and White is not going to let us know.
Do they all cuddle or sit in a huddle? Who knows, but here is a theory . . .
Being snug and warm is considered the norm, if you're a Norwegian fairy.

The Old Lady's Cat up a Tree

There was an old lady in Surrey,
Whose cat got stuck up a tree,
So she phoned for aid from the Fire Brigade
As quickly as quick could be.

Half an hour later they screeched to a halt,
And proceeded with training inborn
To go through their drill efficiently, till
There were hose pipes all over her lawn.

The old lady cried 'No, no, my cat
has been stuck up that tree all day',
So Fireman Spadder shot up a ladder,
Where all he could think of to say . . .

. . . was 'Pussy, come 'ere, little pussy,
And I'll stick you back down on the deck'.
The pussy just purred quite undeterred
So he grabbed the scruff of her neck.

The firemen cheered and the old lady wept
When he reached the base of the tree.
Her eyes were misted as she insisted
The firemen must stay for tea.

The old lady plied them with biscuits and cake,
Hot scones and sandwiches too,
But they had to hurry as the rest of Surrey
Had more urgent jobs to do.

They climbed back on to their shiny machine
And the old lady waved her hat,
As they drove down the track, the firemen waved back,
Which is *when* they ran over the cat!

The Old Toms' Cat Gut Band

At the back of Bradbourne Terrace,
On the garden wall they stand,
And every night you can hear the sound
Of the Old Toms' Cat Gut Band.

They've killed off all the other Toms,
Who started to get out of hand,
And now their guts make up the strings
Of the Old Toms' Cat Gut Band.

There's a Ginger on the viola,
Fallon scraping the fiddle,
Ed's a disgrace at twanging the bass
And Jasper sings in the middle.

Bogo's plucking the cello,
Jumbo is on the guitar,
But Bertie is only allowed to play
A tennis racquet so far.

Local residents hate the noise,
And windows are often slammed,
But no one around can dampen the sound
Of the Old Toms' Cat Gut Band.

If you want a request they'll do their best,
It's Ed who generally slots it,
But the only song they know by heart
Is 'Memories' by Andrew Lloyd Wotsit.

Puma

The Puma is the mountain lion of the U.S.A.;
No other cat can jump as far to pounce upon its prey.
One leapt across the Grand Canyon while carrying Dick
Van Dyke,
Which is more than can be said for E. Knievel on his bike!

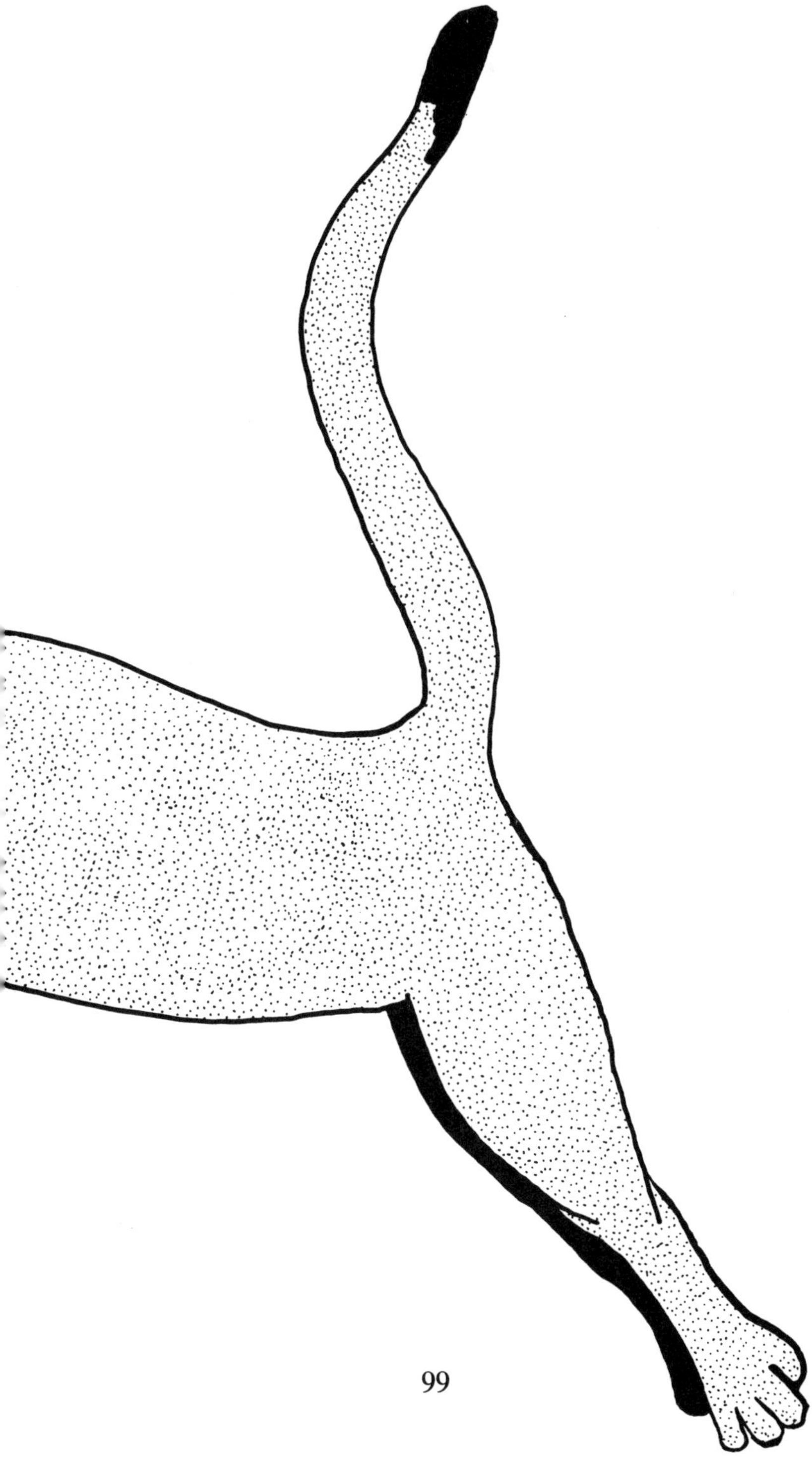

Ragdoll

Ragdoll, Ragdoll, what a funny name
And a white Persian Queen is the one who is to blame.
She was in a road crash that gave her such a scare,
That little Ragdoll kittens were littered everywhere.

Ragdoll, Ragdoll hasn't any fear,
But won't get in a fight, anytime or anywhere,
Does a horrid road crash properly explain
Why Ragdoll kitty cats cannot ever feel a pain?

Ragdoll, Ragdoll maybe that is why,
You live in California, hoping bye and bye
Some producer will believe that your story is so good,
That a feature film called *Ragdoll* will be made in
Hollywood.

Richard the Leopard

Richard the Leopard hunts by night from the bough of
an African tree,
Waiting for monkeys, small antelope and also I fear for *Me*.
So I hung up a bait of chicken, that was riddled with
chicken pox,
But it didn't fool old Richard, 'cause he'll never change his
spots.

I tried to bait him regularly with various morsels of meat,
But every night he stayed in the tree and never came down
to eat.
Then I cooked a plum duff pudding, which strangely
enough did the trick.
So Richard has managed to keep his spots, but he fell for a
'Spotted Dick'.

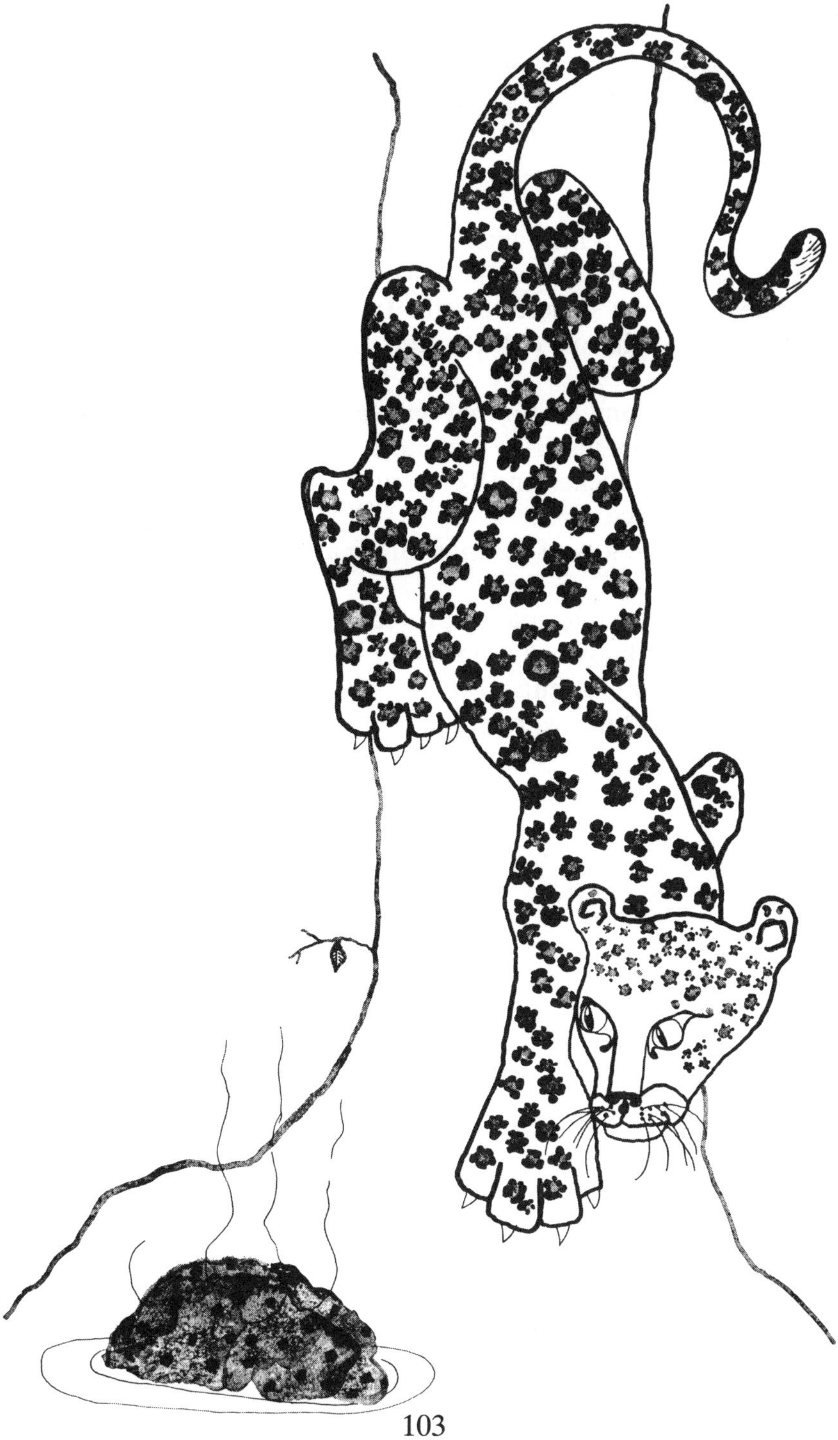

Russian Blues

A green-eyed little kitten in a northern White Sea port,
Where the icy Russian blizzards blew and blew,
Appeared to be so cold that the frozen sailors thought
That they ought to call the kitten 'Russian Blue'.

When they found a ship that was sailing off to France,
The frozen Russian Blue was stowed away.
The freighter docked in Brest and the kitten grabbed his chance . . .
Now there are lots of Russian Blues around today.

They have a double coat to protect them from the weather,
But we don't know what goes on inside their heads.
Are they double agents? I often wonder whether
The Russian Blues were planted by the Reds.

The Scratching Post

When Tricia bought a scratching post
Her cats were fairly certain,
They were supposed to scratch the post
Instead of Tricia's curtain.

Instead of Tricia's tablecloth
And chair material too,
Instead of climbing up the wall
To rip the paper through.

But even after three months' training,
Her cats can safely boast,
They've ruined Tricia's furniture
But never touched her post.

Shimra the Persian White

Shimra the long-haired Persian White
Appears on the telly every night,
Promoting food for cat's delight.
Shimra's star is burning bright.

Being long-haired, she's very fluffy,
And being a Persian, awfully stuffy,
But underneath she's quite a toughie;
Call her 'Puss' and she'll get huffy.

Shimra's beauty makes hearts throb,
And lots of toms would love the job,
But she won't mate with any slob.
Shimra is a dreadful snob.

But Persian Shimra sometimes hollers,
'I will give a million dollars
To any cat or man who collars
All those blinking Ayatollahs'.

Siamese Seal Point

If you want a loving cat, that tries so hard to please,
You needn't look much further than the Seal Point
Siamese;
Loyal and affectionate, I'll take an even bet
You'll never find a cat that's a better household pet.

You can teach her to do somersaults and also to retrieve;
With patience any trick she will eventually achieve.
I wouldn't recommend that you use a flying trapeze,
But nothing is impossible to Seal Point Siamese.

As for Seal Point beauty, her eyes are piercing blue.
Her mask, her tail and ears are brown and also stockings
too.
Her coat, of course, is cream, but you mustn't be perplexed
If she disappears at night, 'cause she's highly oversexed.

Yes, the Seal Point Siamese is a flirty little flitter,
And at *only* six months old will produce a full-sized litter.
To Siamese it's natural and shouldn't be a shock,
When you think of all the naughties practised nightly in
Bangkok.

Skimpy the Stray?

Skimpy is a greedy cat who lives at No 7,
Where she's fed on Rabbit's liver which is her idea of
heaven.
She purrs beside her mistress, indicating 'Liver's fine',
Then she nips out through the cat trap to No 39 . . .

. . . whose owners think that she's a stray and wouldn't
ever dream
Of denying the darling kittie a saucerful of cream.
Skimpy laps it slowly till there isn't any more,
Purrs a bit to show content, then off to 44.

Outside the door of 44 she miaows until she's heard,
A man yells out 'That stray is back, this really is absurd'.
His wife is full of pity for a cat that's out so late,
So she chops up little titbits and puts them on a plate.

Mrs Bowles at No 5 always lets her in,
But Skimpy's very fussy about eating from a tin,
So she lies beside a hole in the kitchen of the house,
And regular as clockwork out pops a little mouse.

Then back to No 7 to sleep away the day,
The other owners wait till night to welcome back their
'stray'.
The routine still goes on, so I mustn't be too catty,
But she ought to change her name from 'Skimpy' into
'Fatty'.

3 4 5 6

Somali

The ruddy brown Somali has a ruddy bad opinion
of people who insist that she's a ruddy Abyssinian.
Truth be known the tie between their breeds is very strong,
But Somalis have a coat that's a ruddy sight more long.

Somalis have 'ticked' coats, and they have 'ticked' hairs by
the score,
So do Abyssinians but Somalis much, much more.
And when they blow their noses they always use a
tissue . . .
A normal sign of manners, taught in downtown Mogadishu.

So forget the Abyssinians, they're a ruddy sight too snarly,
Quite unlike the calmness of the ruddy brown Somali.
And if the reason *why* they're gentle leaves you at a loss,
When you're very ticked, you won't get ruddy cross.

Sugar

Sugar, a San Francisco cat,
While climbing a tree, had a slip.
She was rushed to the vet where the x-ray showed
She'd slightly deformed her left hip.

But Sugar still adored to climb
And she loved her owner Fay Brown,
So all was OK until one fine day,
When the Browns had to move out of town.

Mr Brown had to settle in Tulsa,
On account of his getting promotion,
But sadly they had to leave Sugar behind;
To move her was too much commotion.

They fostered her out to a friend nearby;
They knew she'd be loved and looked after;
But three weeks later the friend rang them up:
Sugar had done a clean scarper.

Fay Brown was distraught in Tulsa,
She prayed to God for his pardon.
Six months went by when she heard a small cry;
It was Sugar out in the garden.

By now she looked pretty bedraggled
From her over twelve hundred mile trip.
There was no doubt at all it was Sugar,
With her slightly deformed left hip.

How did Sugar know where to go,
And survive on the journey too?
Well the Browns still live in Tulsa
And the story's entirely true.

WASHINGTON
Portland
OREGON
MONTANA
NORTH DAKOTA
SOUTH DAKOTA
IDAHO
WYOMING
Cheyenne
NEVADA
CALIFORNIA
San Francisco
UTAH
COLORADO
Denver
NEBRASKA
KANSAS
TULSA
OKLAHOMA
LOS ANGELES
ARIZONA
San Diego
Phoenix
NEW MEXICO
BAJA CALIFORNIA
Sonora
CHIHUAHUA
TEXAS
MICHIGAN
WISCONSIN
DETROIT
IOWA
Des Moines
CHICAGO
ILLINOIS
INDIANA
OHIO

Tabatha Queen of the Night

Tabatha, Tabatha, where can you be?
The night is too cold to be hiding from me.
Under a rosebush or way up a tree,
Tabatha, come home to me.

Tabatha, Tabatha, always the same,
The night is too wet to be playing a game.
If you catch pneumonia I get the blame,
Tabatha, answer your name.

Tabatha, Tabatha, though I adore
The sound of your purr and the touch of your paw,
I'm getting soaked outside the back door,
Tabatha, don't be a bore.

Tabatha, Tabatha, I'm going to bed,
So you'll have to climb through the window instead.
And if you are covered in scars that have bled,
Tabatha, tears will be shed.

Tabatha, Tabatha, sleep very tight,
Wherever you are I'm saying goodnight.
I pray in the morning you'll still be all right,
Tabatha, Queen of the Night.

Talek the Cheetah

Talek is a cheetah in the Mara Game Reserve,
And if you watch him carefully two things you will
observe.
He's either lying motionless low down in the grass,
Or sprinting like he's got a turbocharger up his ass.

For Talek is a cheetah and nothing can run faster;
At 400 yards he is the absolute past master.
For the innocent impala, the warthog or gazelle,
If Talek gets a whiff of them, they're on their way to hell.

He races them and trips them, then he grabs them by the
throat,
And if tripping seems unfair we humans shouldn't gloat,
For remember we're imprisoned for such a simple slip,
As lighting up the Grass before a way-out trip.

Talek is so fast, he kills far too many deer
And when he does, quite suddenly, a Warden will
appear . . .
'Talek you're too greedy and I'm tired of all your pleading
Sixty miles an hour, mate? I'm nicking you for speeding'.

So now the little Dik Diks are all breeding in the park.
You can hear the mating call of the over-sexed Aardvark,
But as they multiply fourfold, Talek's keeping track
Of the days that still remain till he gets his licence back.

Tara the Tiger

Tara the Tiger's daily meals are boring chunks of meat,
But she recalls her father saying how grandpa used to eat:
A Bengal Lancer for breakfast, a Dhobi Wallah for lunch,
And a tea planter for Tiffin with a Maharajah to munch.

For the biggest cat on earth there isn't much to do
When you're stuck inside the cage of a European Zoo,
Being goggled at all day by a bunch of human cranks,
Making *Essoteric* quips about 'Tigers in their Tanks'.

But Tara has a dungeon where she lies against the wall,
And dreams of gaining freedom in the jungles of Nepal.
There's little chance of that, but she's not a heavy sleeper,
So instead she plots the day when she'll gobble up her keeper.

Tinkle Bell

Tinkle seems a gentle cat, her owner's pride and joy.
She purrs around the house, looking very very coy;
But isn't *quite* so gentle when she's put outside the door –
She always brings a bird back and drops it on the floor.

Sometimes it's a robin, sometimes it's a swallow,
Once it was a pigeon with a cuckoo's chick to follow.
Her owner was enraged so to save the birds from hell,
Around the neck of Tinkle, he hung a little bell.

Tinkle Bell, Tinkle Bell, she thought it most absurd,
And found it very difficult to catch a blinking bird.
But being a very clever cat she lay and watched them all,
And noticed that a chaffinch liked to sing from on the wall.

She waited till it flew away, the silly little finch,
Then crept below the wall where she didn't move an inch.
Pretty soon the finch came back and merrily he sang.
Tinkle kind of liked the tune, but all the same she sprang.

Tinkle Bell, Tinkle Bell, gone and dropped a clanger;
Chaffinch on the kitchen floor . . . owner full of anger.
Any scheme to save the birds a cunning cat soon wrecks.
You'll never save the birds by hanging bells around their
necks.

Turkish White Angora

The Turkish White Angoras are long-haired, sleek and slim,
And are blessed with a fantastic ability to swim.
They swam across the Bosporus – I swear that isn't bull,
To get from Asia Minor into naughty Istanbul.

That was before the bridge was built but nowadays for laughs,
Angoras swim at least four lengths in local swimming baths.
They excel at relay races and they always time the splits,
And you *must* remember Munich, the Angoran Mark who Spitz?

Now they're training hard, 'cause they want to see their names
In the 1988 World Olympic Games.
Unless the local Asian food causes diarrhoea,
I expect them to win Gold in the baths of South Korea.